A Broken Rose

by
Sarah Goddard

Playdead Press

Published by Playdead Press 2012

© Sarah Goddard 2012

Sarah Goddard has asserted her rights under the Copyright, Design and Patents Act, 1988, to be identified as the author of this work.

A CIP catalogue record for this book is available from the British Library.

ISBN 978-0-9572859-4-1

Caution

All rights whatsoever in this play are strictly reserved and application for performance should be sought through the author before rehearsals begin. No performance may be given unless a license has been obtained.

This book is sold subject to the condition that it shall not by way of trade or otherwise, be lent, resold, hired out, or otherwise circulated without the publisher's prior consent in any form of binding or cover other than that in which it is published and without a similar condition including this condition being imposed on the subsequent purchaser.

Playdead Press
www.playdeadpress.com

Sarah Goddard set up Five One Productions after graduating from the University of York in 2009. After two successful years at the Edinburgh Fringe, Five One debuted in London, collecting five Off West End Offie Award nominations for Three of Hearts at the Etcetera in Camden, including Best New Play and Most Promising New Playwright. A Broken Rose is her 12th play.

Five One Productions was started in 2009 by Sarah Goddard. The company aims to produce solely pieces of new writing. With fourteen productions over the last three years at the Edinburgh Fringe, and four in London, this new company has started strong. Five One are based in London.
www.five-one-productions.com.

The author would like to thank Hoxton Hall, The Cockpit Theatre, K & K Stationers, Super Hire, The National props hire, Kevin Wilson and all those involved in this production who have allowed it to come to life!

A Broken Rose was first performed at the Cockpit Theatre, London on 11th September 2012. The cast was as follows:

Maria	Louisa Lytton
Jess	Nicola Wright
Dr. Cole	Nick Boulton
Sun	Amy Barnes
Moon	Chris Barley
Johnny	John Last

Director	Phil Willmott
Assistant Director	Eyal Israel
Set/Costume Designer	Emma Tompkins
Stage Manager	Lauren Baxter
Lighting Designer	Becca Sharpe
Costumes	Natasha Mackmurdie
Original Music	John-Paul Bowman
Casting Director	Danielle Tarento
Photography	Scott Rylander
Producer	Five One Productions

A Broken Rose

by
Sarah Goddard

CHARACTERS:

MARIA

JESS

COLE

JOHNNY

SUN

MOON

Act One, Scene I:
1970s. The stage is divided in half, with a table and chairs on one side and Maria's room on the other. The Fairy, Sun stands in the wing and sings as she slowly enters. Maria is lying on the floor. Moon slowly enters from the opposite side.

SUN (Sings) A tale of flowers, a tale of gold
An ancient tale by ancients told
Of our young maid and of her plight
A girl by day and a queen by night
She travelled the lands in the walls of her room
In spirit she fled from her terrible tomb
And she reigns in the land of the gold
And she reigns in the land of the gold
At night when we came she started awake
And begged us to from her confines take
For she was lost to ice and dark
And her young eyes were losing their spark
We heeded her wishes but it had a price
Her honour be proved to our peoples thrice
And she reigns in the land of the gold
And she reigns in the land of the gold
And then at the last when she brought us the babe
An innocent's life for all sins repaid
With courage she took him and brought him to me
And all of her honour our people could see

> So then from the shadows her breathing was ceased
> Her spirit at last from its tomb was released
> And she reigns in the land of the gold
> And she reigns in the land of the gold

Moon picks up a coat and assumes the guise of Maria's father.

MOON　　　Shall we start with a story?
SUN　　　　Like the ones her father told her every night.

Moon takes up Maria and lies her down so she seems to be lying in bed, awaiting a story.

MARIA　　　Which story are you going to tell tonight, daddy?
MOON　　　Which one would you like to hear?
MARIA　　　Something exciting!
MOON　　　Aren't they all exciting?
MARIA　　　The one with the dragons. And the prince and the princess.
MOON　　　Yes, and then you'll keep us up all night with your nightmares.
MARIA　　　A new one then.
SUN　　　　And he told her a story of a faraway land.

MOON	Once upon a time, far away, in a land where few little girls had ever dared to venture.
SUN	In a land of flowers and gold.
MARIA	Is this story about me?
MOON	Well you'll never know if you keep interrupting will you?
MARIA	Lips zipped!
MOON	Good. And in this faraway land, everything was glinting with gold and diamonds. All the girls had flowers in their hair and the sun had to shine behind clouds all the time because otherwise his reflection on the gold would blind everyone. But though it was cloudy, the sky was bright and glistening.
MARIA	Was everything really made of gold?
MOON	And diamonds.
MARIA	Is there going to be a prince?
MOON	This is a different kind of story.
MARIA	What kind of story?
SUN	How you love your stories.
MOON	The princess was to be entrusted with a great responsibility.
MARIA	She must have been very brave and very wise.

Enter Jess, looking haggard and worn. Slightly drunk.

JESS	Who are you talking to?

MARIA   Daddy's telling me a story.

Moon immediately loses the disguise as Maria remembers her father has died.

JESS   Your daddy's dead Maria. Don't be a fool. You're nearly fourteen. It's time to stop these silly games.
MARIA   Yes, mother.

Moon and Sun stand to the side as Johnny enters and grabs Jess up in hug and kisses her passionately, indifferent to the fact that her daughter is in the room.

JESS   *(Exasperated)* I've missed you so much.
MARIA   *(To Sun and Moon)* Not him again.
JOHNNY   What's it to you? *(Thinking Maria is talking to him.)*
JESS   Don't mind her. She can't tell what's real and what's in her silly little head.
SUN   *(Indicates who Jess is. To Moon)* Jess used to love Maria. But three years ago, when her father was killed in a car crash—
MOON   Things weren't the same.
SUN   Jess was never the same again.
MOON   *(Indicates who Johnny is)* Johnny is spending an increasing amount of time in the house.
MARIA   *(To Moon)* You sounded just like my dad you know.

MOON	We fairies have little powers like that.
MARIA	Can other little girls see you too?
SUN	We've been sent especially to you. Nobody else can see us.
MARIA	Why me? I'm not important.
MOON	Well you must be. It isn't every day we get sent to a human child.
SUN	She won't be a child for much longer.
MARIA	That's what mother keeps saying.
SUN	What do you mean?
MARIA	She says I'm too old for silly stories.
MARIA	I liked your story.
MOON	I'm glad.
MARIA	What was the princess's responsibility?
SUN	You'll soon learn, Maria.
MARIA	Do you come from the land in the story? The one that's made of gold and diamonds.
MOON	And flowers.
MARIA	And flowers?
SUN	We do come from that land, yes. But we've been gone for a long time.
MARIA	Why?
SUN	We've been looking for you, Maria.
JESS	Maria, go play in your room.
MARIA	I'm not sleepy yet.
JESS	Go to your room.
JOHNNY	Forget it, let's go down the pub.
JESS	We're going out Maria.

Scene II:
Maria goes with the fairies to her room. Jess and Johnny exit.

MARIA	Johnny's here a lot now.
SUN	Yes.
MARIA	But he's not my real father.
MOON	We know that.
MARIA	If you've been looking for me, and you come from that magical land far away from here, can't you take me there with you?
SUN	Outsiders aren't allowed now. Ever since greedy humans arrived with great carts to fill with gold and carry away.
MOON	The King and Queen had to do something.
SUN	Or their beautiful kingdom would be ruined forever.
MOON	So they sealed off the lands. No one can enter or leave the kingdom unless they know the spell. And the Royal Family has vowed to keep it that way as long as they live.
MARIA	What if they die?
SUN	In order for the Royal Family to live forever and keep the kingdom safe, the young princess has to capture innocence.
MARIA	Capture innocence? What does that mean?
SUN	We're hoping the princess can tell us. But nobody can find her.
MARIA	Is she missing?

MOON	The king sent her away for her own protection before she was even born.
MARIA	Where did he send her?
SUN	I took her from the land. I brought Moon with me. We journeyed to Earth, where we left her in the womb of a human being. She would live in that family, as a mortal. But she would always be half-fairy.
MOON	And she doesn't know her true parents, nor of the kingdom they came from. She doesn't know how to capture innocence to keep the Royal Family and their kingdom safe.
SUN	Well. We need to find that child.
MARIA	How will you find her?
SUN	It will be difficult. She'll look like all other human children. There will be no distinctive mark on her, so we've been looking at all the little girls that are of the right age.
MARIA	There must be millions.
SUN	Yes. But only she will be able to see fairies.

Pause

MARIA	Is this story about me?
SUN	You can see fairies, Maria.
MOON	And you are the correct age. We think you're the daughter we carried away nearly fourteen years ago.

SUN	We need your help.
MARIA	I get to be a princess? In the land of gold and diamonds and fairies?
SUN	That's what we hope.
MARIA	Then please take me with you. Take me away from here.
SUN	We will, but first you must fulfill your destiny. You must learn how to capture innocence. Are you strong enough for that task?
MARIA	I... I think so.
MOON	There will be three challenges along the way to test your strength and fortitude. But we'll be with you Maria, and we will guide you.

The fairies exit.

Scene III:
Maria is onstage alone. Jess and Johnny are being noisily intimate next door. Maria puts her hands over her ears and sings.

MARIA	(Sings) A young princess lives in a faraway land
	Away from the terrors she can't understand
	Away from a mother who hates all her past

> Away from the shadow that was over her cast
> With fairies she'll live and with fairies she'll reign
> And forget all the pity and all of the pain
> Her father revived through his magical tales
> In a land where all goodness and kindness prevails
> And she'll reign in the land of the gold
> And she'll reign in the land of the gold

Exits

Scene IV:
Jess drunkenly sways onstage in her underwear humming the song her daughter was just singing. Johnny stumbles in after her. They waltz around until suddenly Moon appears, in the guise of the father again, and Jess is dancing with him and Johnny interchangeably. The scene gets confused. Maria enters.

MARIA Mother?

Jess continues between the two 'men' and eventually slumps down against Johnny who starts touching her again.

JESS Not in front of the girl.
JOHNNY Send her away then.
JESS Maria, go to your room.

MARIA	You thought you were dancing with daddy.

Johnny laughs at her.

JOHNNY	Your girl's insane, Jess.
MARIA	I'm not insane. And I'm not deaf.
JOHNNY	Lippy as well? Go to your room.
MARIA	I saw you! I saw you dancing with Daddy!
JOHNNY	Oh here we go again.
JESS	*(To Maria)* Be quiet.
MARIA	You know you were. Why won't you admit it? I saw you!
JESS	He's gone Maria. You need to accept that.
JOHNNY	Seriously. She needs some help.
JESS	I'll deal with it Johnny.
MARIA	You're drunk.
JOHNNY	Had a few too many pills, more like.
JESS	Go to your room.
MARIA	No. You can see them too.
JESS	See what?
MARIA	Fairies.
JOHNNY	For fuck's sake.
JESS	Grow up Maria.
MARIA	Who were you dancing with then?
JESS	Johnny.
MARIA	And when you weren't dancing with him?
JOHNNY	Get out, you're confusing us both.
MARIA	You don't know what you're talking about.

JOHNNY	Thank god for that.
JESS	Leave her alone Johnny. She's not well.
JOHNNY	Damn right she's not well. If you weren't so out of your head you'd sort it out.
JESS	Go to your room.
MARIA	What have you taken mother?
JESS	Go to your room!
JOHNNY	Listen to your mother. Or I'll make you wish you had.

Starts to exit.

JESS	Johnny, please.

He stays.

MARIA	I hate you. I hate you both.
JOHNNY	*(Less harshly)* Just go to your room.

Maria hesitates but starts to exit. Moon and Sun watch, disgustedly, from the sides. They comfort her. Johnny starts kissing Jess and is lying on top of her but Jess is too far gone to respond. He doesn't stop.

MARIA	Get off her!
MOON	You can't do anything now, Maria.
MARIA	I hate him.
MOON	But your mother does not.
SUN	She should do.
MARIA	He's not my father.

SUN	He'll never be your father. Come away now.
MARIA	No.
SUN	Come on. You shouldn't see this.
MARIA	It's disgusting. He's disgusting.
SUN	Yes. But there's nothing you can do now.
MARIA	I could get him off her.
MOON	He's too strong for you.
MARIA	How can you just let this happen? He's not too strong for you. What's wrong with you?
SUN	This isn't our problem.
MARIA	But it's mine.
SUN	I know it is. Remember we said there would be three tasks as you prepare yourself?
MARIA	To capture innocence?
MOON	That's right.
SUN	Your first task will be to protect your mother. But not now. When I command it.
MARIA	So I'm supposed to just watch this happen? And wait for whenever you feel like stepping in. I thought you were good fairies.
SUN	We are. And you will wait.
MARIA	What if I don't?
SUN	Then you'll never capture innocence and return with us to the land of the gold. You will remain a simple mortal human with

these disgusting creatures for the rest of your days.

Exits. Maria starts to cry.

MOON	Listen to what she has said. It'll all make sense in time.
MARIA	It isn't fair.
MOON	You wouldn't prove your worth if the tasks did not challenge you.

Scene V:
The next morning. Jess and Johnny sit at the table. As Maria enters, Johnny walks out without saying goodbye. Jess is just in a dressing gown.

MARIA	You should put some clothes on.
JESS	You should shut your mouth.
MARIA	Are you still drunk?
JESS	I wish. Get me a drink.
MARIA	No.
JESS	Fine. *(Gesturing to the flowers on the table)* How long how these been here?
MARIA	Since yesterday. I picked them from the garden. Do you want me to get you your clothes?
JESS	Why bother?
MARIA	It's cold.
JESS	Whatever.

Maria exits. Jess picks up an old photograph.

JESS *(To the photograph)* Why the hell did you leave me like this? You and your fucking stories. She believes them still and I'm left to pick up the pieces. You shouldn't have done that to me.

She goes to the corner and throws the picture away. Then pulls a cigarette out of her pocket and tries to light it. Maria returns with her clothes.

MARIA You shouldn't smoke.
JESS You shouldn't believe in fairies.
MARIA You saw them too.

Jess slams her hand on the table.

JESS Enough! You're getting ridiculous. It isn't real.
MARIA Maybe you just don't want it to be real.
JESS Give me those.

Maria hands her the clothes and she starts to dress. There are bruises on her body.

MARIA What are those from?
JESS I fell over.
MARIA It's him isn't it? Just get rid of him mother. I don't like him.

JESS	You don't know what you're talking about.
MARIA	Nor do you.
JESS	Shut up.
MARIA	You look awful.
JESS	I'm not feeling well.
MARIA	Then you definitely shouldn't smoke.

She takes away the cigarette.

JESS	What did I do to deserve you? Get out of my sight.

She is starting to sway.

MARIA	Are you alright?
JESS	Go away. Mother doesn't want her little spawn to annoy her anymore.
MARIA	I'm not your spawn. I am the only heir to the throne of the land of the gold. Half of my blood is that of a fairy and I will live forever.
JESS	For god's sake fairies aren't real!
MARIA	They are. And they don't like you.
JESS	Poor me. Go to your room.
MARIA	You look sick.
JESS	I'd look better if you left me alone!

She vomits. The fairies enter.

MARIA	*(To the fairies)* I'm going to help mother get better. I can look after her. I can clean up and look after her.
JESS	For god's sake Maria!
MARIA	It's alright mother.
JESS	You were talking to yourself.
MARIA	No I wasn't. Now you should go to bed and I'll clean up this mess.
JESS	Johnny was right.
MARIA	I doubt it.
JESS	You are a freak.
MARIA	And you're a drunk. At least I can control myself.
JESS	What by talking to your fairies? You need to grow up. You're not a little girl anymore. It's not cute.
MARIA	Neither is being sick all over the kitchen.
JESS	I'm going back to bed.
MARIA	Good.
JESS	I don't need this. I don't need to deal with you.
MARIA	Fine.
JESS	Clean up this mess.
MARIA	Sleep well mother.

Jess exits. Maria gets a bucket of water and a cloth and begins to clean.

MOON	You don't have to do this.
MARIA	It will smell.

MOON	No child should have to see her mother behave like that.
SUN	No child should have to lose a father. She is doing well.
MARIA	Tell me a story, Daddy.
MOON	Which story would you like to hear?
MARIA	I don't care.
SUN	It isn't really your father, Maria.
MARIA	You think I don't know that? Do it anyway.
SUN	Don't speak to Moon like that.
MARIA	Please.
MOON	It's alright.
SUN	Watch your tone Maria. We are here to make you Queen remember.
MARIA	Yes. And if I don't do exactly as you say I get left here.
SUN	We have your best interests at heart.
MARIA	Whatever you say.
MOON	A story, then?
MARIA	Please.
MOON	Well. Once upon a time there was a magical flower. This flower was magical because whenever it bloomed, it released oils that gave all those that touched them magical powers.
MARIA	*(Crying as she cleans)* What kind of magical powers, Daddy?

Sun shakes her head and exits.

MOON		The oils would grant them one wish.
MARIA		Just the one?
MOON		Just the one. And people would come from all over the world to try and touch this flower. But it was guarded by a forest of densely growing trees. The trees were old and wise, and they knew the dangers of having wishes granted, so they prevented any man or woman from getting to the flower. Until one day, a man came to the edge of the forest, and whispered what his wish was to the trees. Amazingly, they let him pass.
MARIA		What was his wish?
MOON		He approached the flower. It was blooming and radiant in all its beauty. He rubbed the luscious petals between his fingers and the oils flowed out, grateful that they could finally be used. And the man made his wish.
MARIA		And? She is nearly finished cleaning.
MOON		And the flower died.
MARIA		Why?
MOON		Because the man was clever, and knew that wishes could only bring disappointment. He wished the flower's magic would disappear, and as it did, the flower wilted and died. Leaving him to clamber his way back through the forest to

	spread the word that there was no longer any need to have false hope.
MARIA	That's a sad story.
MOON	Yes. But I hope you were listening.
MARIA	I know you aren't really my father.
MOON	Good.
MARIA	And I'm never going to let Johnny make my mother sick like that again.
MOON	You don't have that power, I'm afraid.
MARIA	I'll protect her.
MOON	At the bidding of Sun.
MARIA	Yes. Beat. If I do complete my tasks and go and live in the land of the gold with the fairies, will I be happy?
MOON	For the rest of your days.
MARIA	Then I'll do whatever it takes.

They exit.

Scene VI:
Jess is lying on a sofa asleep.

MARIA	She's sleeping.
MOON	Doesn't she look peaceful?
MOON	Why don't you tell her a story?
MARIA	I don't know any I can tell. And she'll just get angry.

Enter Sun. Sound of door opening and Johnny clambering about.

SUN	Johnny is coming.
MARIA	But she's asleep.
MOON	Maybe he'll go away.
SUN	No. This is it, Maria. I command you, in order to prove your honour to our people, to protect your mother.
MARIA	*(Frightened)* Is he angry?
SUN	He's drunk.
MARIA	I'm frightened.
SUN	Here *(Hands her the bunch of wildflowers she finds on the table. They are wilted and their colours have faded.)* Take these. The smell should calm him. Or ward him off.
MARIA	What?
SUN	Either way your mother will be protected.
MARIA	He's so much bigger than I am.
MOON	Listen to Sun. You can do this.
SUN	Remember what is at stake. You can do this because you must do this.
MARIA	I remember.

Enter Johnny. Maria stands tall, holding the flowers in front of her, bracing herself.

JOHNNY	Wake up.

Jess starts to wake.

JESS	I'm not well.
JOHNNY	Do I look like I care?

MARIA	Go away Johnny.
JOHNNY	Where did you come from? Haven't you learned you aren't wanted?
MARIA	I'm warning you.
JOHNNY	Sorry… you're warning me? Are you hearing this Jess? Your kid's gone and threatened me.
JESS	Johnny she's just a girl. I was sick.
JOHNNY	I don't give a fuck.
MARIA	She won't see you today.
JOHNNY	She's seeing me right now. Now get out. This is grown-up time.
MARIA	I know what you do in your grown-up time. She's got bruises on her.
JOHNNY	Has she now?
MARIA	And I know she didn't fall over.
JOHNNY	Are you sure about that? Because your mother's a drunk. Drunks fall over all the time. All sorts of accidents happen to them.
MARIA	And I know when they're not accidents.
JOHNNY	You need to learn to listen, girl.
MARIA	You need to leave. Mother isn't well today.
JESS	Maria, do as he says.
JOHNNY	Coming to her defence now are you?
JESS	She doesn't understand.
JOHNNY	What's there to understand? She's thirteen Jess. She's not a little girl anymore.
JESS	She is in her mind.

JOHNNY	In her mind she plays with fairies. She's fucking sick.
MARIA	You need to leave now.
JOHNNY	Are you hearing this? I'm not going anywhere. *(He climbs onto the bed.)*
JESS	Johnny, please. I'm not feeling well.
JOHNNY	I don't like to repeat myself.
SUN	Are you ready?

Maria nods, terrified.

MOON	Wait for our signal.

Johnny starts undressing Jess.

JOHNNY	I don't mind a fucking audience!
MARIA	Just leave!
JESS	Maria go to your room.
JOHNNY	You be quiet; she obviously isn't going to listen.
JESS	She shouldn't be here.
JOHNNY	Never been more right in your life.
MARIA	Get away from my mother. Now.
JOHNNY	Get lost, Maria.

His hand moves under the blanket.

JESS	Please, she's just a girl.
JOHNNY	And it's about time she grew up.

MARIA	I'm warning you, Johnny, you need to leave now!
JOHNNY	I've just about fucking had it with you.
JESS	Go to your room Maria, please.

He holds her down with his other arm and kisses her.

SUN	Now.

Maria rushes forward and pulls Johnny off the bed, bristling the flowers at him as she goes. He is both shocked and disturbed. And then angry.

JOHNNY	What the hell?
MARIA	I warned you to stay away from her!
JESS	Maria what are you doing?
JOHNNY	What the fuck is wrong with you? *(He slaps Maria.)* Now get out of here.
JESS	Johnny!
JOHNNY	She isn't made of glass. I don't need this; I'm leaving.
MARIA	Don't come back.
JOHNNY	I have to come back. How do you think you can have such nice things? And food and clothes?
JESS	Johnny, please.
JOHNNY	Nice little arrangement, we've got.
MARIA	Get out.
JOHNNY	*(To Jess)* I could almost call you a whore.
MARIA	Out!

JOHNNY	I'll be back when you're feeling better.

Exits.

SUN	Your task is complete. You've proved your honour to us.
MARIA	And look at what's happened!
SUN	You bore it well.
JESS	Maria…
MARIA	I protected you, just like they asked.
JESS	Maria fairies don't exist! Whatever they've told you to do. What good has it done? You've been hit and I've been humiliated. Do you do everything these fairies tell you?
MARIA	They would never hurt me.
JESS	You stupid girl. You stupid, stupid girl.

Maria turns, but Moon and Sun have gone.

MARIA	I protected you.
JESS	You made a dangerous man angry. That's not protection.
MARIA	One day you'll thank me.
JESS	You aren't well Maria.
MARIA	He called you a whore.
JESS	People say all sorts of things when they are angry.
MARIA	He didn't say all sorts. He said you were a whore.

JESS	Stop saying it.
MARIA	Is it true?
JESS	No. He loves me. You've just upset him. I'm going to get you a doctor.
MARIA	I'm not sick.
JESS	Yes you are. And I'm sick of this fairies nonsense.
MARIA	It isn't nonsense.
JESS	Your daddy ruined you.
MARIA	I wish he were still here.
JESS	Well he's not. And he'll never come back to us. Now leave me alone.
MARIA	I'm sorry you don't believe me, mother. *(Faces audience)* But one day I won't be here anymore, and then you will know that I am with the fairies in a magical land far, far away from here. Where the streets and grounds are all made of gold and diamonds. And the sun has to shield itself behind clouds to protect the eyes of the people who live there. I will be a princess, and I will never return to this place.

Jess looks exasperated as she covers her face with her hands. Blackout.

Act Two, Scene I:
Doctor Cole stands ready to enter. Jess goes to meet him.

JESS	You must be Dr. Cole.

COLE		Yes. Nice to meet you.
JESS		Thank you. I'm Jess. Please sit down.
COLE		Thank you. *They move into the scene.*
JESS		I spoke to somebody else on the phone.
COLE		Yes, my secretary I presume.
JESS		Oh. I was expecting a woman.
COLE		I don't think my gender will be a problem.
JESS		No. Right.
COLE		It's quite common for parents to be a little apprehensive at this stage.
JESS		I'm not. I just don't know what to do.
COLE		Where's your daughter?
JESS		Maria. She's probably in her room. Do you want me to get her?
COLE		Not for now. We'll have a chat about everything first, and then I can get her side of the story.
JESS		Well that's exactly what it is Dr. Cole—
COLE		Frank.
JESS		Frank. A story. That's all that she believes in.
COLE		Often children who have experienced a great deal of grief or trauma at an early age will attempt to compensate with their imaginations.
JESS		Yes. Her father was killed in a car crash when she was ten.
COLE		Is that when the stories started becoming more real for her?

JESS	Yes. But she loved those stories even then. He told her a different story every night, though I always thought she was far too old for bedtime stories. And some of them gave her nightmares.
COLE	But did she ask for them?
JESS	Sometimes. I think it was just a habit neither of them wanted to break.
COLE	I see.
JESS	Are you married Frank?
COLE	No.
JESS	It's hard work.
COLE	What do you mean?
JESS	I mean she was meant to be my little girl, you know? You always see mothers and daughters walking around, holding hands and laughing. I wanted her to be my best friend. Like you always expect mother and daughter to be. But she was his best friend. Father and daughter.
COLE	Do you think you were jealous?
JESS	Probably. I don't understand the obsession with stories. They aren't real.
COLE	Well that is exactly the appeal sometimes.
JESS	She wasn't a little girl anymore. It was getting silly.
COLE	Just because she enjoyed hearing them doesn't mean she didn't know they weren't real.

JESS If that were the case we wouldn't be having this conversation.

COLE True. But that might've developed later. When her father was no longer there to create the stories.

JESS Maybe.

COLE How did her behavior change after his death?

JESS I don't know.

COLE You don't know?

JESS I wasn't really paying attention.

COLE You were a grieving wife.

JESS She just stayed in her room all the time.

COLE Did you try and speak to her?

JESS Of course I did! I was a damned good mother.

COLE What changed?

JESS She didn't want any of my stories.

COLE I'm sure she just associated stories with your husband.

JESS She didn't want to talk to me full stop.

COLE You don't know that.

JESS She'd rather talk to her imaginary fairy friends.

COLE Yes. Which story were those from?

JESS I don't know.

COLE Did you read stories as well?

JESS No. He made them up. But I don't know of any fairies like that in his stories.

COLE Like what?

JESS	She talks to them all the time now. And says they tell her what to do. She attacked my boyfriend with a bunch of flowers.
COLE	It wouldn't be unusual if she didn't take kindly to a new man in the house.

Pause.

COLE	Is she frightened of him?
JESS	She didn't seem to be then.
COLE	And she says the fairies told her to do that?
JESS	Yes. She said she was… protecting me.
COLE	I see. Does she have any friends? Other children she plays with?
JESS	No. I've been home schooling her since her father died. She was being bullied.
COLE	She doesn't see other children her age at all, then?
JESS	No. We don't get out much.
COLE	Do you think the fairies could be replacing those?
JESS	Probably. She thinks she's some kind of princess.

Maria enters.

MARIA	Hello.
COLE	Hello.
MARIA	I'm Maria.

COLE	I know. I'm Frank.
MARIA	Are you mother's new boyfriend?
JESS	Maria!
COLE	No, I'm a doctor.
MARIA	Well I'm not sick.
COLE	I'm not here to give you any medicine.
MARIA	Then you don't sound like a very good doctor.
JESS	Be polite.
MARIA	Sorry.
COLE	It's alright. Would it be alright if I spoke to you for a little while?
MARIA	Why?
COLE	Your mother tells me you have some interesting friends.
MARIA	You want to tell me they don't exist as well?
COLE	No. I want to learn all about them.
MARIA	And what if I don't want to tell you? You're talking to me like a baby.
JESS	I'm sorry. She's not used to company.
MARIA	He is though.
COLE	No, she's right. How old are you Maria?
MARIA	Nearly fourteen.
COLE	Then I shall speak to you accordingly.
JESS	Nearly fourteen and still believing in silly stories.
COLE	We'll discuss that later.
JESS	Good luck.

Jess exits.

SUN   Alone.
MARIA   What do you really want?
MOON   You can say whatever you want.
SUN   She's not here anymore.
COLE   I told you. I want to hear about your fairies.
MARIA   So you can tell me they don't exist?
COLE   No. So I can learn about them.
MARIA   Mother thinks I'm crazy.
COLE   I don't think you're crazy Maria.
MARIA   Even though I can see fairies?
COLE   Even though.
MARIA   Well I can see them now. They're sitting right here. Their names are Moon and Sun and they brought me here before I was born.
COLE   To live with this family?
MARIA   Yes. Can you see them?
COLE   I can't.
MARIA   Oh. Sometimes I think I'm the only one. But sometimes I think mother can see them really, she just doesn't want to.
COLE   You think she can see the fairies?
MARIA   Moon is very good at disguising himself. He sometimes looks like my father. I saw them dancing together. But she was drunk.
COLE   I see.

MARIA	She's drunk a lot of the time. Sometimes not drunk. Sometimes something else like it though.
COLE	This is with her boyfriend?
MARIA	*(Hesitates)* Yes. Sometimes just her though.

Pause.

COLE	You like stories, don't you Maria?
MARIA	I love them.
COLE	Do you think you could tell me one?
MARIA	You want to hear a story?
COLE	I do.
MARIA	What kind of story?
COLE	Hmm how about a bedtime story?
MARIA	Are you sleepy?
COLE	Nope. Just want to hear a bedtime story.
MARIA	Why?
COLE	I love stories too.
SUN	Tell him a story then.

Jess enters and listens unseen.

MARIA	Ok. Um.
MOON	Don't be afraid.
MARIA	I'm not afraid.
COLE	You don't need to be, Maria. I just want to hear a story.
MOON	Go on.

MARIA	Well. All stories start with 'Once upon a time…' That's what daddy always said.
COLE	Wise man.
MARIA	The wisest. Once upon a time there lived a little girl who lived in a little hut in the forest.
MOON	Why did she live in a hut?
MARIA	She lived all alone in a hut because her father had died and her mother had gone away. And because she was on her own, she started to make friends with some of the animals in the forest. The little rabbits and deer. And the birds that sang sweetly in the trees.
MOON	She could talk to the animals?
MARIA	They understood that they each meant no harm to the other and that they were friends. Then one day, an old woman came to the hut. The little girl thought she might be a witch, so when she asked to come in, she turned her away. She was all on her own after all. And she was right to be suspicious, because once she turned her away, the woman cast a terrible spell over the house.
MOON	What happened?
MARIA	Um. Well the house no longer welcomed the little girl, and she was cast out into the forest. And because she had been so unkind to the witch, none of the creatures

	of the forest would help her. And she had taken her voice, so she couldn't even communicate with the animals.
COLE	How sad.
MARIA	Yes. But that isn't the end.
COLE	Ok.
MARIA	The girl soon grew accustomed to her wildlife surroundings. She didn't need to talk after all when there was nobody or no animals to talk to. After a time, the girl got older. She built a new house for herself in the treetops. And a new woman approached and asked to come in. This time, the girl had learned, and allowed her in. When the woman entered, she saw that it was her mother, unchanged over all the years, but somehow sadder and with greying hair at the temples. To her horror, she saw that the woman was blind, and she would never recognise her. She embraced her mother nonetheless, and even in her blindness, the woman felt an old familiarity in her touch. The two lived on in the treetops for the rest of their lives, in mutual love, but the mother never knowing that she was with her daughter once more.
COLE	Thank you Maria.
MARIA	Did you like the story?
COLE	Very much. Where did you hear that one?

MARIA	Nowhere. I made that one up. I started telling one that daddy had told me, but I couldn't remember it. I can't remember any of his stories now. Not unless Moon tells them to me. Like I said, he can do a good disguise.
COLE	And when Moon tells you the stories, do you know it isn't really your father?
MARIA	Yes. I don't want to. But I do.
COLE	You're very grown up for your age, Maria.
MARIA	Well you're the only person who thinks that.
COLE	How many people do you tell you stories to?
MARIA	No one. Sometimes when mother is sleeping I tell her one, but she never wakes up.
COLE	Well thank you for telling me one.
MARIA	You're welcome. You aren't like normal doctors.
COLE	No?
MARIA	They don't listen to me.
COLE	I'm a different kind of doctor.
MARIA	Will you come back again?
COLE	Yes. I will be back very often.
MARIA	To see mother?
COLE	To see you.

Enter Jess, straightening herself out.

JESS	Thank you Dr. Cole.
COLE	Not at all. Are you alright?
JESS	Quite fine, yes. Did you enjoy that, Maria?
MARIA	I liked it more than normal doctors.
JESS	Maria doesn't like injections.
COLE	Well I'm not one of those doctors.
MARIA	Can I go back to my room now?
JESS	Yes.
COLE	See you soon.
MARIA	Bye.

Maria exits. The fairies follow.

COLE	She did well.
JESS	Yes.
JESS	It was a sad story.
COLE	She's a sad girl.
JESS	What about the fairies?
COLE	Your daughter's not insane, Jess. She's just grieving.
JESS	But she sees them. Really sees them.
COLE	And as she grows up, she'll realise that she doesn't see them as well as she thinks she does now. But she needs you.
JESS	I know.
COLE	I'll see you soon.
JESS	Do I pay now?
COLE	No. The first session is just an assessment. The next will be a paid one.
JESS	Thank you.

COLE Take care. I'll see myself out.

Cole exits. Jess sniffs and straightens out her hair and clothes.

Scene II:
Jess stares at herself in the mirror. She goes to a wardrobe and pulls out a nice evening dress and drapes it against herself, then she puts it on. She takes off her heavy makeup and fixes her hair. The fairies are watching her. Moon goes over and kisses her cheek. Jess reacts as if she's felt it and touches the place on her face and keeps looking in the mirror. Then she crosses the stage and goes to join Maria.

Scene III:
Maria is sitting with a book open and reading. Enter Jess from the other room followed closely by Sun and Moon. Maria is stunned by her mother's appearance.

JESS Did you enjoy your time with Dr. Cole?
MARIA It was ok. Is that why you were smiling?
JESS Don't be ridiculous.

Maria shrugs.

JESS He'll come three times a week. Hopefully you'll start to realise that you're just far too old to believe in half the things you do.
MARIA And then what? What do you believe in?
JESS I don't really believe in anything.

MARIA	That isn't possible.
JESS	I'm not really the religious type.
MARIA	Love?
JESS	Don't be stupid Maria. You can't put your faith in love or trust or anything like that.
MARIA	I do though.
JESS	Then you're weaker for it.
MARIA	You loved daddy.
JESS	Don't talk about that.
MARIA	Do you love me?

Pause.

JESS	I'm your mother. I feed you and house you. I school you. I teach you that stories are stories and real life is real life. Anything else would weaken us both.
MARIA	I don't love you either.
JESS	I need a drink.
MARIA	You want a drink.
JESS	Yeah. She pours herself a glass of wine.
MARIA	I'm sorry Johnny called you what he did. *(Jess shrugs.)* I don't believe it. But I'm sorry you are that to him.
JESS	You don't understand things like that Maria. All you understand is what your little fairies tell you.
MARIA	I understand a lot more than that. They teach me more than you ever did.
JESS	Lucky you.

MARIA	Yes.
JESS	One day you'll realise that these voices in your head are poisoning you. Then those fairies might not look so beautiful.
MARIA	And one day you'll realise I want more than feeding and housing.

Jess continues to drink. The fairies come into the scene. Maria is upset.

SUN	You don't have time to worry about what she says.
MOON	You still have two tasks to carry out.
MARIA	But I still have to protect her.
MOON	Of course.
MARIA	I don't know if I can do that one anymore. So why should I bother with the others?
SUN	So you choose to forsake your people. You'll live here and die here as a mere human. You have failed us! We brought you here and now we've come to take you back and save the land we once loved, and you repay us with laziness. These are not the words of a princess. These are the words of a frightened little child.
MARIA	I'm not frightened! And I'm not a little child.
SUN	No? And yet you can only complete one of a mere three tasks.

MARIA	She doesn't want protecting. I can't stop her drinking and it's making her sick every day. I can't stop her from seeing Johnny.
SUN	And when have you tried to do either of those things?
MARIA	I always try.
SUN	Try harder.
MOON	We're so disappointed in you Maria.
SUN	You have let us all down.
MARIA	You haven't even given me a chance. If you're here to help me, why don't you help me? I've never felt so alone since you arrived.
SUN	They're your tasks, not ours. And we did help you. We gave you the flowers.
MARIA	And I got slapped.
SUN	We didn't say the tasks would be easy. We just didn't expect you to be such a coward.
MARIA	I'm not a coward.
SUN	Well I'm not convinced of that. Come, Moon. There's nothing for us here.
MARIA	You're just going to leave me here?
SUN	You've failed us Maria.
MARIA	Give me another chance.
SUN	You'll fail us again.
MARIA	You don't know that.
MOON	Tell Dr. Cole the truth.
MARIA	About what?
SUN	Everything.
MARIA	And that's the second task?

SUN	Yes.
MARIA	But that's easy!
MOON	Tell him the truth about everything, and you will prove your honour to us.
MARIA	I will.
SUN	We'll be watching you.
MARIA	I won't let you down.
SUN	We shall see.

Sun exits.

MOON	This is your final chance, Maria. If you fail you'll stay here in this world. And you'll never see us again.
MARIA	I understand.
MOON	Good luck.

Moon exits.

Maria hums 'Land of the Gold' and returns to her mother in the other room. Jess is getting more and more drunk. She has spilled drink all over her lovely dress and is attempting to put on her makeup again without a mirror. She looks a mess.

MARIA	You've got wine all over your dress.
JESS	Who cares?
MARIA	That's the dress daddy loved so much. You've ruined it.
JESS	It'll wash.

MARIA	It's wine. You always say wine doesn't come out.
JESS	Leave me alone, Maria.
MARIA	I was wondering when Dr. Cole was next coming.
JESS	Oh you want him to come now?
MARIA	I never didn't.
JESS	Either tomorrow or the next day. I said I'd let him know later.
MARIA	I don't think you should phone him just now.
JESS	And why is that? I'm perfectly capable of booking my daughter an appointment with her shrink.
MARIA	Shrink?
JESS	Psychiatrist. Whatever.
MARIA	So he's that kind of doctor.
JESS	What did you think he was? Maria you spend half your day talking to fairies. It's annoying.
MARIA	You think I'm crazy.
JESS	I think talking to him will prove either way.
MARIA	I think you should talk to him.
JESS	I only see things that are really there.
MARIA	Most of the time.
JESS	What's that supposed to mean?
MARIA	You never used to drink like this. I think it's because of daddy.

JESS	Don't you ever say that again. You don't understand anything!
MARIA	I want to see him tomorrow.
JESS	Fine. Bring me the phone.

Maria stands alone.

MARIA Tell me a story Moon. Or Sun. I would like to hear a story. *(Pause)* You aren't here, are you?

The fairies do not appear.

MARIA Once upon a time. I will tell a story. And then you say 'all great stories must begin with "once upon a time"'. Once upon a time there was a little girl who wanted to go and live with the fairies. 'Why would she want to do that' you say. She wanted to go and live with the fairies because her life was making her very sad. 'What was so sad about her real life?' Well she soon realised that her mother was very sick. And there was nothing she could do to make her better. And her fairy friends all left because she let them down. 'Will they come back?' you say. (Pause.) But I don't know if they will. I can't let them down again.

Scene IV:
Enter Dr. Cole.

COLE	Is your mother around?
MARIA	She's upstairs with Johnny so I'm all on my own again. I expect she's forgotten you were coming.
COLE	Where are your friends?
MARIA	They're gone.
COLE	Oh?
MARIA	They asked me to protect my mother and I did. But I couldn't continue to. She's sick all the time. And now they've left and punished me.
COLE	I'm sure they will come back. How have they punished you?
MARIA	I don't want to talk about it.
COLE	I need you to be honest with me Maria.
MARIA	I know. I need to be honest with you as well.
COLE	Good.
MARIA	Sun got angry. I think that must have been what it was.
COLE	What what was?
MARIA	I started... bleeding. It's never happened before, so I must have made them very angry.
COLE	Where were you bleeding?
MARIA	It was on my sheets when I woke up this morning.

COLE	Has your mother ever spoken to you about anything like that Maria?
MARIA	She says they don't exist.
COLE	I mean the bleeding.
MARIA	No. I don't think she would believe me. I washed the sheets. She won't know. It's disgusting.
COLE	It's perfectly normal Maria.
MARIA	It's never happened before.
COLE	It starts to happen when little girls become young women. It isn't because the fairies are angry with you. So you don't have to worry about that.
MARIA	I don't?
COLE	No. I'm sure they'll come back to you soon. When you need them back they will come.
MARIA	And then will the bleeding stop?
COLE	Soon. But it will happen again. You should speak to your mother about it.
MARIA	I'd rather speak to you.
COLE	Not about something like that. How did you enjoy our first meeting yesterday?
MARIA	It was ok.
COLE	Did you like talking to somebody about the fairies?
MARIA	I liked that you didn't make fun of me.
COLE	I will never make fun of you Maria. I brought you something today, actually.
MARIA	Like a present?

COLE Yes.

He takes out a big book of Grimm fairytales.

MARIA I love books!
COLE Then I think you'll love this one especially. It's all made up of fairytale stories. And it has beautiful pictures.
MARIA Thank you.

She thumbs through it happily.

COLE You should see if your mother will read some to you.
MARIA I can read.
COLE But she might like to read them as well.
MARIA My mother doesn't like stories.
COLE I see.

Jess crosses and exits.

MARIA Johnny's not her boyfriend, you know.
COLE No?
MARIA No. The last time he was here he told me he pays her. He's not a nice man.
COLE It's possible you just misunderstood. Sometimes things aren't as they seem.
MARIA I'm not a child.
COLE I know you aren't.
MARIA Is that how she pays you?

47

COLE	Of course not.
MARIA	She said you're a psychiatrist.
COLE	I am.
MARIA	So does that mean I'm crazy?
COLE	No.
MARIA	Well I can't see them anymore.
COLE	Is that because they've gone away or because they aren't here now?
MARIA	I don't know.
COLE	Do you want to see them again?
MARIA	Yes. But not when they're angry.
COLE	Were they frightening?
MARIA	Very. They said I'd have to stay here forever.
COLE	Instead of going back to live with them.
MARIA	Yes. They said I wasn't behaving like a princess. I was behaving like a coward.
COLE	Sometimes when we're angry we say things we don't necessarily mean.
MARIA	I know that. But I don't want to get stuck here.
COLE	I think you'd miss your mother very much.
MARIA	You don't know my mother.
COLE	No. But I know she would miss you.
MARIA	How?
COLE	I don't see my son very often. And I miss him all the time.

MARIA	So go and see him more. If she doesn't bring Johnny she can probably come and see me in the land of the flowers and gold.
COLE	Your mother is probably still very sad about losing her husband.
MARIA	She doesn't seem to be. I'm not allowed to talk about it.
COLE	People deal with grief in different ways.
MARIA	She drinks a lot and wears too much makeup.
COLE	It takes time to heal.

There is a faint crash from offstage. Dr. Cole doesn't seem to think anything of it, but Maria is suddenly alert. Enter Moon.

MARIA	*(Warily)* Moon!
COLE	Have they come back?
MARIA	Just Moon.
MOON	You are doing well Maria. But now you need to protect your mother.
MARIA	Why?
MOON	Just do as we say.
MARIA	She's with Johnny.
MOON	Yes.
COLE	What's Moon saying?
MARIA	I have to protect my mother.
COLE	Maria—

There is a shout and we can hear Jess crying and Johnny shouting and swearing at Jess. Dr. Cole is confused as Maria seemed to know her mother was in danger before the sound.

COLE	Stay here.
MARIA	How can we just stay here?!
COLE	I'll go.
MARIA	I have to protect her. It's my task to!

Jess comes running into the room. Her mouth is bleeding, she is crying, and she is holding a pregnancy test.

JESS	Please.
MARIA	Mother?
COLE	What's happened?
JESS	He's angry and he's had a lot to drink. He doesn't know his own strength.
MARIA	Moon? Moon has vanished.
JESS	He just panicked that's all.

Johnny bursts in. Dr. Cole shields Maria. Jess cowers.

JOHNNY	Get rid of it.
JESS	I can't.
JOHNNY	What do you mean you can't? I won't have it.
COLE	I think you need to leave, Johnny.
JOHNNY	Who the fuck are you?
COLE	I'm the family doctor.

JOHNNY	*(To Jess)* Are you screwing him as well? Is it his brat?
JESS	No!
MARIA	What happened?
JESS	I'm pregnant.
JOHNNY	You're the family doctor and you missed that?
JESS	He's not the family doctor, he's Maria's psychiatrist. I'm sorry Johnny I just thought you should know. I won't ask for anything.
COLE	Maria maybe you should go to your room.
MARIA	I have to protect her.
COLE	This isn't the time to protect your mother.
JOHNNY	You sure as hell aren't asking for anything.
JESS	I'm sorry.

Cole moves between them just as Johnny is about to hit Jess again.

JOHNNY	This is none of your business.
COLE	You will not touch her again. I'll phone the police.
MARIA	Or I will. Get out Johnny.
JOHNNY	You going to come and hit me with some fucking daisies, kid?
COLE	Maria, the phone.
JOHNNY	Alright, alright.
COLE	Now.

JOHNNY	I'm going.

He gives Cole a shove and exits. Cole and Maria go to Jess.

JESS	I'm sorry. He just doesn't know his own strength.
MARIA	I tried to protect you mother. I said he shouldn't come back.
COLE	Are you alright?
JESS	I'm pregnant.
COLE	Is it his?
JESS	Of course it is.
MARIA	He can't be a father.
JESS	Maria, please. You don't understand.
COLE	Has he hit you before?
JESS	It's fine. It's barely anything.
COLE	There's a lot of blood.
JESS	It's fine.
MARIA	He shouldn't come back.
JESS	He has to come back. I can't…
MARIA	He doesn't care about you.

Enter Sun and Moon.

SUN	Maria.
MARIA	I can't talk to you now.
SUN	We understand that.
COLE	Are the fairies back now?

Jess starts to cry.

MARIA	They know I need them here for me.
JESS	Please, Frank. Just go. I'm sorry you had to see this.
MARIA	I don't want him to go. (To Cole) Can't you be the baby's daddy? You don't see your son very often.
JESS	Maria, don't be stupid.
COLE	I'm sorry Maria I can't do that.
MARIA	Why not?
COLE	I am just a doctor.
MARIA	But you like me, don't you? I could be your daughter.
JESS	I'm sorry, she's just upset.
COLE	I do like you. Very much, Maria. You're a special little girl. But I can't be your father. And I think you know that.
JESS	We'll be alright. There's no need for you to do anything else.
COLE	Let me know when you'd like me to come back.
JESS	It's fine. Thank you.
COLE	Goodbye Maria.
MARIA	See you soon. Thank you for the book.
COLE	You're welcome.

Cole pats Jess on the arm and leaves. Jess suddenly clings to Maria. She is on the ground and Maria is standing. Jess cries and Maria strokes her head.

MARIA	I'm sorry he hit you mother.
JESS	We'll be fine Maria. We'll be fine.
MARIA	What are you going to do?
JESS	Why don't you tell me one of your stories?
MARIA	I thought you didn't like stories.
JESS	I'd like to hear one now.
MARIA	Ok.
JESS	Thank you.
MARIA	Once upon a time there lived a beautiful maiden, and she had the sweetest singing voice in all the lands. She loved music and dancing and everyone who knew her loved her. One day the sound of her singing drifted into the stables and the little farm boy heard the beautiful notes. He fell in love instantaneously but he knew he could never be with her. He could not sing a single tune, and the maid was renowned for her love of music.

The fairies sit around them and listen.

> One day he came across a terrible witch, and he begged her to help him in his plight. She asked if he would love her if she could no longer sing, and the boy hesitated. He said he loved her voice and that it was so much a part of her that he could not love her without it. The witch smiled and said she would grant him the

54

	talent of song but it would come with a price.
JESS	What was the price?
MARIA	The boy ran to the maiden's house, singing so sweetly as he went. He knocked on the door and found himself in front of the face behind the lovely sound he had heard in the barn. He was so excited to finally see her that he did not notice the saddened look in her eyes, and burst enthusiastically into a beautiful love song. But the girl only stared at him. For the boy had been selfish in his wish, and it had left his love deafened, never again to hear the music she loved so dearly.

Jess looks up at her daughter for the first time. Maria stares straight ahead, completely immersed in the story. Blackout.

Act Three, Scene I:
A few months have passed. Jess is now visibly pregnant. But other than that it appears little has changed. We see her sitting at the table with a glass of wine, despite the pregnancy. Maria is lying on the ground on her front reading the Grimm book. There is a knock at the door. Jess goes to answer it. It is Dr. Cole.

JESS	Dr. Cole?
COLE	Maria phoned my office.
JESS	I see. I'm so sorry about what happened.

COLE	Are you alright?
JESS	We're fine, now. I hadn't realised it had been so long since she'd seen you.
COLE	Is it ok if I see her now?
JESS	Of course. She's reading the book you gave her.

They join Maria.

COLE	Which one are you on now?
MARIA	Cinderella. But I've read it three times already.
COLE	Are you enjoying it?
MARIA	Every time.
COLE	They're good aren't they?
MARIA	I like them.
COLE	You shouldn't be drinking, Jess.
MARIA	She knows that.
JESS	Be quiet Maria.
COLE	Is she right?
JESS	You're not the right kind of doctor to give me advice on that.
COLE	I'm human. You're poisoning your child.
JESS	*(Sadly)* Yes.
MARIA	What are we going to talk about today?
JESS	Yes. This session is for Maria. I have to go.
COLE	I'm sorry, it wasn't my place.
JESS	It's Johnny's child. I will see you afterwards.
COLE	See you then.

Jess exits. Maria looks after where her mother has gone, thoughtful.

COLE (*Awkwardly*) So what would you like to talk about?

MARIA Isn't that your job?

COLE I haven't been for a while, and the last time I was here was a bit different.

MARIA And then you didn't come back.

COLE I wanted to give you both time to sort some things out.

MARIA Nothing has changed.

COLE Surely some things have changed.

MARIA Johnny still comes. Mother still drinks. I still see things that everybody says don't exist.

COLE Are they here now?

MARIA No.

COLE I find them interesting, you know.

MARIA So?

COLE They knew your mother was in danger before we did.

MARIA Because one of my tasks was to protect my mother.

COLE What was the other?

MARIA To be honest with you. And to tell you only the truth.

COLE Have you done that?

MARIA I think so.

COLE	So you've got one task left.
MARIA	Yes.
COLE	You don't seem very excited.
MARIA	I think it'll be the most difficult.
COLE	But then you get to go with them.
MARIA	If I succeed.
COLE	Do you think you won't?
MARIA	I think I'm a coward.
COLE	You're not a coward Maria.
MARIA	I was meant to protect. I haven't. Johnny still comes, and she's still too blind to see what he does to her.
COLE	Has he ever hurt you?
MARIA	Only when I tried to get between them. That was my first task.
COLE	It isn't any of my business, but—
MARIA	No. It isn't. You're meant to come here and spend time with me. Not mother.
COLE	I'm just concerned Maria. That's all.
MARIA	She likes you, you know. A lot. She never used to dress nicely, and she does more and more since you left. Just in case you came back.
COLE	I think she doesn't want me to think certain things about her.
MARIA	But you think them anyway, don't you?
COLE	I barely know your mother.
MARIA	You know she drinks too much even though there's a baby in her. You know what Johnny calls her.

COLE	What Johnny calls her is an incredibly horrible thing.
MARIA	That doesn't mean it isn't true.
COLE	Maria.
MARIA	You haven't been here. It's been six months and you haven't been here at all.
COLE	I don't belong here, Maria.
MARIA	Yes you do, you do belong here because you need to speak with me. Nobody speaks with me.
COLE	I'm sorry.
MARIA	No you're not.
COLE	I'm here now. And I'll be here whenever you need me.
MARIA	You're just a doctor.
COLE	I am, yes. But I'm also your friend.
MARIA	You don't know what it was like.
COLE	No.
MARIA	I thought things would change. I really, really did. She wanted a story. I told her a story. Sun and Moon were there and they were smiling at me. But nothing changed. She finished crying, lit up a cigarette and didn't speak to me for nearly a month. A month! It's just the two of us here you know. A month is a long time.
COLE	Imagine how lonely she must have been. At least you had Sun and Moon to keep you company.

MARIA	I did yes. But every time I spoke to them I felt like I was betraying her.
COLE	Why did you think that?
MARIA	She had nobody.
COLE	Did you try talking to her?
MARIA	Yes. She ignored me and drank more. Even when I said it would hurt the baby, she kept drinking. Or she would go to her room and slam the door in my face. She hates me.
COLE	She doesn't hate you.
MARIA	Just because I told her a story. I reminded her too much of daddy.
COLE	You think that was what it was?
MARIA	That's what Moon thinks. And it isn't fair. Nobody told me these things would happen to me, or my body. I didn't know what was going on. I wanted a mother and I needed her and she wouldn't talk to me. I just had to guess.
COLE	I'm sorry Maria.
MARIA	It doesn't matter if you're sorry.
COLE	No. I understand that you feel like that.
MARIA	You don't understand anything. I bet all the time you've been here you've just been trying to figure out what's wrong with me. You're not listening, you're just trying to fix me and be done with it.
COLE	That isn't true at all. I'm listening because I'm interested, and because I care.

MARIA	You aren't my father. That's a father's job. You're just a doctor.
COLE	I can't be your father Maria. And he's gone. All I can be is your friend, and I think you could do with a few more of those.
MARIA	Yes. My own age. Or not fairies. But where can I get those?
COLE	Friendships can be blind to ages.
MARIA	I never leave the house. Do you know that? She's embarrassed by me. Says people don't need to see me talking to myself in the streets. But I'm not talking to myself. I'm talking to my friends and I can see them because I'm special, not because I'm crazy.
COLE	That's how they know you're the princess.
MARIA	Exactly.
COLE	Why haven't given you a task all this time?
MARIA	I don't know. It makes me feel forgotten.
COLE	I'm sure you aren't forgotten.
MARIA	How would you know? You can't even see them.
COLE	You're their princess. They need you.
MARIA	True.
COLE	If you call out to them, do they come?
MARIA	Sometimes. It depends on how I'm feeling.
COLE	What do you mean?

MARIA		If I'm really angry, they come, but if I'm alright and just bored, they know there are better things they could do with their time. But sometimes I just like talking to them.
COLE		I understand.
MARIA		They still tell me bedtime stories though.
COLE		I'm glad to hear it.
MARIA		Yeah. People always say I'll grow out of it. I'm fourteen now.
COLE		That's still very young.
MARIA		But I'm starting to think they're right. I've just been waiting and waiting for the next task, and nothing comes. And when I ask Sun she tells me that princesses are always patient.
COLE		Aside from the final task, what else are you waiting for in your life? Maybe it'll coincide with that.
MARIA		I'm not waiting for anything other than to get out of here.
COLE		I see. I'll miss you when that does happen.
MARIA		When? So you think I'll do it?
COLE		I have full faith in you, Maria. If the fairies think you can be their princess then I'm sure you can.
MARIA		They think I can be their princess because I am their princess. I didn't have to achieve anything to be that. I was just born.

COLE	But they think you can rule them as Queen.
MARIA	Yes.
COLE	They must have some faith in you then.
MARIA	I suppose. Why do you always ask about the fairies?
COLE	I've never met somebody who can see them before.
MARIA	No other crazy little girls you see?
COLE	I still don't think you're crazy.
MARIA	Well I'm not special either. I'm sure there are thousands of children who have fairy friends. The only difference with me is that I can really see them.
COLE	And you don't think the others can?
MARIA	They even call them imaginary friends.
COLE	True.
MARIA	My fairies are not imaginary. They are real. I can see them, and I'll one day live among them.
COLE	Then you're a lucky girl.
MARIA	Sometimes I think so too. But I have to live through this world first.
COLE	*(Concerned)* Why do you say that?
MARIA	It doesn't matter.
COLE	Your mother is speaking to you now though.
MARIA	Yes. Not happily.
COLE	Well, however begrudging it may be, it's better than nothing. For both of you.

MARIA	I don't know about that.
COLE	When did Johnny start coming back?
MARIA	He never stopped coming back.
COLE	Even after we threatened to call the police?
MARIA	He knew you would leave. And he knew I wouldn't do it.
COLE	Why wouldn't you do it though? Surely you want to.
MARIA	Mother would definitely hate me then. And there are things in the house she doesn't want seen.
COLE	I see.
MARIA	Do you think she's a bad person?
COLE	I think she's a troubled person. But not a bad one no.
MARIA	I think she's a bad person. She's damaging her baby. And she's already damaged her first baby. She drinks too much and she acts like an idiot.
COLE	She's very sad as well though.
MARIA	Being sad doesn't mean you can ruin other people. I think she's ruined me, though she says my daddy did.
COLE	Ruined you?
MARIA	Yes. Because he told me too many stories.
COLE	The stories are who you are, Maria, and that's nothing to be ashamed of. You know they're just stories, and you know

	you prefer them to real life. That's not crazy. Or ruined.
MARIA	Do you think I'm a bad person?
COLE	No.
MARIA	Sometimes I want to do things I know I shouldn't.
COLE	Like what?
MARIA	Stupid things.
COLE	To your mother?
MARIA	No. But sometimes, when I'm by my bedroom window upstairs, I want to go out of it.
COLE	And jump?
MARIA	And fly.
COLE	Can you fly?
MARIA	No.
COLE	Then that isn't a good idea is it? You'd break a few bones at least.
MARIA	That's sometimes why I want to do it.

Pause.

COLE	Maria, you should never want to harm yourself, but if you ever do, you need to speak to your mother or me about it.
MARIA	I would never actually jump. I just want to sometimes.
COLE	Do you want to do any other things?
MARIA	I sometimes want to hit Johnny.
COLE	I think that's completely understandable.

MARIA	But sometimes I don't. I know he's a bad person and everything, but sometimes… sometimes I want to kiss him.
COLE	Why do you want to do that?
MARIA	I don't know. He hates me so much. But I think I just want to know what it feels like.
COLE	You will one day Maria. But don't ever kiss Johnny.
MARIA	I wouldn't. Have you ever been in love?
COLE	Why do you ask that all of a sudden?
MARIA	The fairies. They tell me how much the King and Queen will love me when I return to their lands. But mother in this world tells me that love makes us weak, and that she doesn't love me.
COLE	I think love can sometimes make us weak yes.
MARIA	So why do people do it?
COLE	You'll understand that one day as well.
MARIA	Who do you love?
COLE	Me? I love my son. I love my family.
MARIA	Could you love me?
COLE	I love you like I love all my clients.
MARIA	Could you love me like you love your son?
COLE	You aren't my son. But you are very important to me, Maria. So don't forget that.
MARIA	What do I have to do to get mother to love me like you love your family?

COLE	I think, deep down, she does already. Your mother is going through a difficult time.
MARIA	It's been years.
COLE	Sometimes it takes that long.
MARIA	I liked the book you gave me.
COLE	I'm glad.
MARIA	The love in those stories is different as well.

Scene II:
Enter Moon and Sun.

MARIA	The fairies are here now.
COLE	What do they want?
SUN	The time will soon come when you'll leave this world, Maria.
MARIA	They say I will leave here soon.
MOON	We have a final task for you.
MARIA	What is it?
SUN	You have already proven your honour to us twice, and for that we are proud of you.
MARIA	Thank you.
SUN	But the final task is the most difficult.
MOON	And we don't expect you to succeed, though we want you to more than anything.
MARIA	What do you want me to do?
COLE	Are they telling you the third task?
MARIA	I think so.

SUN	Do you remember how the royals could be immortal and protect their kingdom forever?
MARIA	Yes. If I can capture innocence.
SUN	Yes.

Pause.

MARIA	You want me to look after the baby when it comes?
SUN	We do. But it's more than that Maria.
MARIA	What else?
COLE	Incredible.
MOON	We need the baby's life.
MARIA	What do you mean?
SUN	We need the child to come with us to our lands, but he will not survive.
MARIA	Why not?
SUN	His blood has been poisoned by his mortal mother.
MARIA	What do you mean?
SUN	The fool shouldn't be drinking alcohol.
MARIA	So what do I have to do?
SUN	When the baby comes, you are to bring him to me.
MARIA	It's a boy?
SUN	It may be. Either way, bring me the child.
MARIA	And you'll save him?
SUN	He's beyond saving. But his blood is the key.

MARIA	The key to what?
COLE	What do they say, Maria?
SUN	The key to our immortality.

Pause.

COLE	Maria?
MARIA	How do I know I can trust you?
SUN	Have we lied to you before?
MARIA	No, but how do I know you won't just leave me behind?
MOON	We can't leave you behind, Maria. You're our princess.
MARIA	I don't know if I can do as you wish.
SUN	We know it's difficult.
MARIA	No. I don't know if I want to.
SUN	*(Reasoning with her)* It won't be a child, Maria. It won't be a person.
MARIA	What do you mean?
SUN	You'll see.
MARIA	I don't want to.
COLE	What are they asking you to do?
MARIA	It doesn't matter.
MOON	It matters hugely.
SUN	Will you do it?
MARIA	I don't know.
SUN	The fate of the world is in your hands, Maria. Your world. Your real world. Please.

MOON	And then we would take you home, where it's normal for people to see fairies, and where you would have more friends than you could know what to do with.
SUN	You must do this.
MARIA	I will try.
SUN	Good. We shall see you soon.
MARIA	Goodbye.

The fairies exit.

COLE	Maria?
MARIA	I know my final task.
COLE	And I gather it's a difficult one.
MARIA	Yes.
COLE	Can you tell me what it is?
MARIA	It's about the baby.
COLE	Your mother's?
MARIA	Yes.
COLE	What about it?
MARIA	In the land where I come from the royals gain immortality if I can capture innocence.
COLE	So… you think the baby might have the innocence you're looking for?
MARIA	Sort of.
COLE	Well you will have a while to wait yet I think, I'm afraid.
MARIA	Why is that?
COLE	Well she isn't due for another two months.

MARIA	I think it won't go to plan.
COLE	Did the fairies say that?
MARIA	In a way.
COLE	Do they want you to do anything that may make that happen?
MARIA	My fairies are good fairies. I won't harm the baby. They said his blood is already poisoned.
COLE	Did you hear your mother and I talking about that earlier?
MARIA	Talking about what?
COLE	How alcohol can poison a fetus's blood?
MARIA	I don't remember.
COLE	Interesting.
MARIA	It isn't interesting. It's frightening.
COLE	Well if the fairies are on your side, surely no harm can come to you or the baby.
MARIA	(Hesitates) Yes.

Scene III:
Enter Jess.

JESS	Are you nearly done?
COLE	Just about. How are you feeling?
MARIA	You need to stop drinking alcohol mother, you will kill your child.
JESS	It isn't my child, it's Johnny's.
MARIA	You're poisoning his blood!
JESS	You mind your own business.
MARIA	That is my business.

JESS	Did you set her up to this?
COLE	No, the fairies talked to her about something.
JESS	Oh so now I'm being advised indirectly by fairies. And I'm supposed to take that seriously?
COLE	I am a doctor and my advice matches theirs.
JESS	You're a psychiatrist.
COLE	It's an innocent child.
JESS	Whatever.
COLE	What's wrong with you?
JESS	How dare you speak to me like that? You're in my house.
COLE	You're poisoning the most innocent form of life.
JESS	*(Short of breath suddenly)* You need to leave. I won't have somebody treat me like this in my own house.
MARIA	You let Johnny in.
JESS	Be quiet Maria.
COLE	She's right.
JESS	*(Passionately)* I've had it with you. You aren't curing my daughter, you're encouraging her! You entertain her little fantasies that fairies exist and are now siding with the fairies against me. Am I the only sane one in this room?
COLE	I am not encouraging her delusions |//
MARIA	Delusions?!

COLE		I am merely working out the cause of them
JESS		I think we all know the cause of them.
MARIA		You said they interested you. You said I wasn't crazy.
COLE		And you aren't Maria, but I have to call them what they are.
MARIA		Delusions are things seen by crazy people.
COLE		You're troubled, you've had a rough few years.
JESS		And her father filled her head with nonsense every night of her life.
MARIA		Don't blame him, he's the only person who has ever loved me!
JESS		*(Softly)* Maria.
MARIA		You're liars both of you.
JESS		Look, you aren't getting any better. You still see these fairies, and it has gone on for far too long now.
MARIA		I see them because they exist.
JESS		I can't see them.
MARIA		You choose not to see them.
JESS		Anyway, Frank, here is your fee. You need to leave now. Johnny is here. Thank you for trying, but I think you've done all you can here.
COLE		Why would you keep me from her?
MARIA		You lied to me.
JESS		She still sees them! You were only hired to stop this nonsense. Certainly not to let it

	continue until you've had your fill of your little experiments.
COLE	It isn't like that at all.
JESS	Just go.
COLE	I believe we were making good headway.
JESS	Well she'll never trust you again now.
COLE	That may be.
JESS	*(Softer)* I'm sorry. It's just best if you go. Maybe we can speak another time on the phone. You don't belong in this mess.
COLE	This mess is my life.
JESS	Just go, please.
MARIA	I'm not sorry I believe in fairies. I'm sorry I believed in you.
COLE	You'll be alright, Maria. Just don't lose sight of the future, and you'll find yourself in the land of the gold, whether that's with the fairies or hidden somewhere in this world.
JESS	Goodbye Frank.
COLE	Goodbye Maria. Goodbye Jess.

He kisses Maria on the forehead. She is starting to cry but tries to look defiant.

MARIA	I hope you remember this for the next poor little boy or girl you look after.
COLE	I will remember this for the rest of my life.

Cole exits. Jess looks as if she wants him to stay. She looks faint, and leans on the table.

JESS I'm sorry Maria but it's for your own good. You aren't well.
MARIA I'm more well than you are. And than that baby will ever be. You've killed it, I know it.
JESS Maria please. Don't talk like that.
MARIA It's just the truth.

Scene IV:
Enter Johnny, carrying a bottle of vodka.

JOHNNY What was he doing here? I thought I told you not to let him in again.
JESS He'll never set foot in this house again.
JOHNNY Damn right. What are you looking at, girl?
MARIA *(Points)* You're bleeding.

Jess has starting bleeding.

JOHNNY Shit.
JESS Oh god.

She sways a little then slumps onto the ground. Sun and Moon enter.

MOON Ask her how it happened.
MARIA What have you done?!

JESS	I would never have a child of yours Johnny.
JOHNNY	What the fuck is that supposed to mean? You're in the third trimester dammit!
JESS	You told me to get rid of it.
JOHNNY	I said that months ago, not now, it's practically a kid now.
JESS	I didn't have the courage before.
MARIA	Mother what've you done?
JESS	Maria call Dr. Cole back.
MARIA	What's he going to do?
JESS	I just want to see him.
JOHNNY	Is that what this is about?
JESS	*(Struggling to get the words out)* This is about me refusing to bring a child of yours into this world.
MARIA	Mother—
JESS	Just do it, Maria!

Maria exits.

JESS	Get out of my house.
JOHNNY	I'll do whatever I please. That's my child!
JESS	Do you normally care for the child of your whore?
JOHNNY	Don't be ungrateful.
JESS	Ungrateful? I have had nothing to be grateful for since Rob died.
JOHNNY	You should be grateful I give you money. You are always needing money. You're too

	fucked up to get up and actually get your own job.
JESS	Who would hire me?

Maria comes back carrying an armful of towels. She lays them about her mother's body.

JESS	Is he coming?
MARIA	He's phoning an ambulance.
JESS	But is he coming?
MARIA	*(Maria nods.)* He's on his way.

Jess gasps.

MARIA	You've killed it mother.
JESS	Maria please stop, it's coming.
JOHNNY	Fucking hell, how did I get stuck in this?!
JESS	Then leave.
SUN	Either she will die or the child or both. Both cannot live.
MARIA	I will do it. I'm sorry mother, I have to complete the final task.
JOHNNY	Not this fairies crap again.
SUN	Remember what we said.
MARIA	I'm frightened.
SUN	It will be alright.
MOON	It isn't a real child.
MARIA	It isn't a real child.
SUN	It's ruined. He is dead.
MARIA	He's dead.

Jess and Johnny run offstage. Jess is crying loudly, Johnny is stomping around swearing. Sun, Moon and Maria join hands and chant:

>A tale of flowers, a tale of gold
>An ancient tale by ancients told
>Of our young maid and of her plight
>A girl by day and a queen by night
>She travelled the lands in the walls of her room
>In spirit she fled from her terrible tomb
>And she reigns in the land of the gold
>And she reigns in the land of the gold

Johnny enters with the baby.

MOON	Remember your task Maria.
MARIA	I don't want to!
SUN	You must.
JOHNNY	What the hell is wrong with you girl?
JESS	*(From offstage)* Where's the baby?
JOHNNY	Don't look at it.
MARIA	I need him.
SUN	We all need him.
MOON	Think of our faraway lands.
SUN	You can do this Maria.
MOON	Your reign needs to be restored.
MARIA	I won't let you down.

Maria reaches out to the body.

JOHNNY   Don't you fucking touch it.

Maria picks up the bundle.

JOHNNY   Let go of it!
MARIA   I have to capture his innocence.
JOHNNY   Let go of it!
MARIA   And now I'll live far away from here forever.

Johnny seems almost mad with anger. He takes the bottle in his hand and swings it hard into the back of Maria's head. Maria falls to the ground and lies motionless.

JOHNNY   *(Horrified at what he has done)* Fucking kid!

Sun goes and stands next to Maria's body. Maria is still holding the bundle. Jess enters, and looks over at the scene, terrified.

JESS   What have you done? She's only a child.
JOHNNY   Come on. We need to get out of here now.
JESS   Don't touch me!
JOHNNY   We need to fucking leave!
JESS   What have you done? What have you done…?

Sun starts singing. As she sings Johnny goes and takes Maria's pulse as well. Moon stays stroking Maria's back. Jess is limp and crying. Johnny tugs at her. He tries to coax her into coming with him, as he knows Maria is dead. Jess won't let go initially. Johnny picks her up and carries her offstage.

SUN	A tale of flowers, a tale of gold
An ancient tale by ancients told
Of our young maid and of her plight
A girl by day and a queen by night
She travelled the lands in the walls of her room
In spirit she fled from her terrible tomb
And she reigns in the land of the gold
And she reigns in the land of the gold
At night when we came she started awake
And begged to from her confines take
For she was lost to ice and dark
And her young eyes were losing their spark
We heeded her wishes but it had a price
Her honour be proved to our peoples thrice
And she reigns in the land of the gold
And she reigns in the land of the gold

Dr. Cole runs on and sees Maria lying on the ground with blood all around her and on the floor where Jess had been lying. He sees the baby, still wrapped up in a miserable bundle. As he enters the fairies retreat, Sun still singing. By the end of the song they are gone. He runs to Maria.

But she paid the price when she brought us the babe
An innocent's life for all sins repaid
With courage she took him and brought him to me
And all of her honour our people could see
But then from the shadows her breathing was ceased
Her spirit at last from its tomb was released
And she reigns in the land of the gold
And she reigns in the land of the gold

Curtain